| DATE DUE | | | |
|---|---|---|---|
| | | | |
| | | | |
| | | | |
| | | | |
| | | | |
| | | | |
| | | | |
| | | | |
| | | | |
| | | | |
| | | | |
| | | | |
| | | | |

*Outlaws and Lawmen of the Wild West*

# WILD BILL HICKOK

Carl R. Green

✦ and ✦

William R. Sanford

**E** ‖ **Enslow Publishers, Inc.**
44 Fadem Road          PO Box 38
Box 699                   Aldershot
Springfield, NJ 07081  Hants GU12 6BP
USA                          UK

**Library of Congress Cataloging-in-Publication Data**

Green, Carl R.
  Wild Bill Hickok / Carl R. Green and William R. Sanford.
    p. cm. — (Outlaws and lawmen of the wild west)
  Includes bibliographical references and index.
  Summary: Chronicles the life of the Western lawman Wild Bill Hickok.
  ISBN 0-89490-366-7
  1. Hickok, Wild Bill, 1837–1876—Juvenile literature. 2. Peace officers—
West (U.S.)—Biography—Juvenile literature. [1. Hickok, Wild Bill,
1837–1876. 2. Peace officers.] I. Sanford, William R. (William Reynolds),
1927– . II. Title. III. Series: Green, Carl R. Outlaws and lawmen of the wild
west.
F594. H62G74  1992
978'.02'092—dc20
[B]                                                              91-29856
                                                                    CIP
                                                                     AC

Printed in the United States of America

10 9 8 7 6

**Illustration Credits:**
Denver Public Library, Western History Collection, pp. 6, 22, 25, 27, 32, 36;
Carl R. Green and William R. Sanford, p. 9; Kansas State Historical Society,
pp. 11, 20, 23, 29, 37; Library of Congress, pp. 17, 39; Stanley J. Morrow
Collection, W. H. Over State Museum, pp. 40, 41; Western History Collec-
tions, University of Oklahoma Library, p. 44.

**Cover Illustration:** Kansas State Historical Society

# CONTENTS

# AUTHORS' NOTE

This book tells the story of a lawman named Wild Bill Hickok. Wild Bill was as famous in his day as rock stars are in our day. People all over the country talked about Wild Bill's adventures. The press raced to print stories about him. Some were made up, but many were true. The events described in this book all come from first-hand reports.

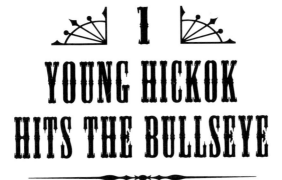

# 1
# YOUNG HICKOK
# HITS THE BULLSEYE

James Butler Hickok was eighteen years old in the spring of 1855. Having just left home he took a job tending cattle in Kansas. When asked his name he answered, "Bill Hickok."

At this time Kansas was about to vote for or against slavery. Bill grew up hating slavery. He wanted to keep Kansas free. But armed men from Missouri were crossing the border to vote for slavery. Colonel James Lane was forming a Free State Army to fight these Border Ruffians.

Bill tried to join Lane's army. An officer smiled and said the army did not take kids. He also said that Lane's men had to own their own horses. Bill did not have a horse. In fact he had only $32 in his pocket. It was a month's pay, but it was not enough to buy a horse.

Lane's army was holding a shooting match on the

*Young Bill Hickok grew up in the rough-and-tumble world of the Wild West. At a time when every man knew how to shoot, Bill's marksmanship helped him make a name for himself.*

edge of town. Bill walked out to watch. The shooting was pretty poor. So Bill paid $30 to enter the contest. That left him only $2, but he had faith in his skill with a gun.

When his turn came he hit the bullseye with his first shot. No one else could match him. In the last event the men aimed at a rolling piece of wood. Bill easily plugged the moving target. The soldiers praised his victory. They said that Colonel Lane needed men who could shoot straight. Bill said he wanted to join, but he did not have a horse. "Yes, you do!" someone shouted. That was when Bill learned that he had won first prize. He now owned a fine bay horse.

Bill soon became one of Colonel Lane's top men. When the general spoke in public, Bill served as his guard. At age eighteen Bill Hickok was fast becoming a gunslinger.

# 2

# WILD BILL GROWS UP

Wild Bill Hickok was born in Illinois on May 27, 1837. William and Polly Hickok named their fifth son James Butler Hickok.

William and Polly came to Illinois from Vermont. As a young man William had studied to be a preacher. He had to change his plans when typhoid fever left him in poor health. He moved his wife and four boys to Homer, Illinois, in 1836. James was born there a year later. Over the next few years Polly also gave birth to two girls, for a total of seven children. On today's maps Homer is known as Troy Grove.

William ran a country store, but lost it in the hard times of 1837. He was forced to make his living as a farmer. Because his health was poor, the boys had to help in the fields. Farm work came before schooling, but Polly made sure that James learned to read and write.

The Hickoks did what they could to fight slavery. William turned the farm into a stop on the Underground Railroad. Runaway slaves hid in the cellar on their way north to freedom in Canada. Young James helped take the blacks to their next hiding place.

By the time James was twelve he owned a rifle and a Colt pistol. When he went hunting the Hickoks could

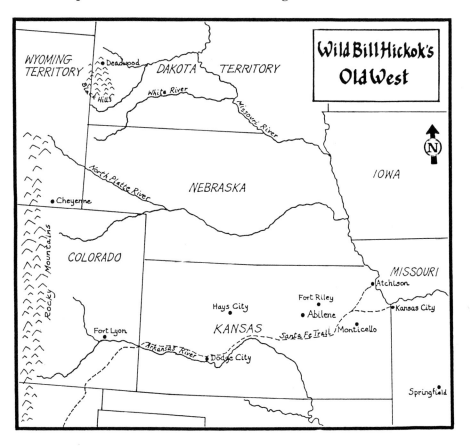

*Wild Bill was born in Illinois, but spent most of his life on the western plains. His greatest fame came in Hays City and Abilene, Kansas. He brought law and order to those tough, lawless towns.*

count on eating well that night. James also made money with his guns. The government was paying hunters fifty cents for each wolf they killed. Because wounded wolves attack their hunters, wolf hunting taught James to make every shot count.

William Hickok died when James was fourteen. By then James's brother Oliver had gone to California. His brothers Horace and Lorenzo helped when they could, but they had their own farms to work. James put meat on the table by hunting deer and rabbits. After a while Polly gave up the farm and moved the few miles back to Homer. James thought town life was boring. He missed the freedom he had known on the farm.

In 1855 James found work as a mule driver. The company that hired him was digging a canal. Before long he was being bullied by an older driver named Charles Hudson. One of Hudson's "jokes" was to push James into the canal. When Hudson did this a second time James fought back. During the wrestling match that followed the two men fell into the canal. Some workers quickly pulled James out of the water. But when they dragged Hudson out he looked dead.

James thought he had killed the bully. He ran home and picked up his clothes and guns. Then he wrote a note to his mother and headed out of town. If he had gone back to the canal he might not have run away. Hudson was still alive.

James walked all the way to St. Louis, Missouri. Then

*Eastern publishers quickly learned that the name Wild Bill Hickok sold magazines. Wild Bill was no stranger to savage fights, but the artist clearly took liberties with the truth in this engraving. Titled "The Struggle for Life," it appeared in an 1867 issue of* Harper's New Monthly Magazine.

he went on to Kansas. There he joined Jim Lane's army and helped make Kansas a free state. For his own reasons James told people his name was Bill. Perhaps he used the name in honor of his father. On legal papers, though, he signed his name, "J. B. Hickok."

By 1858 Bill had grown to just over six feet. He was a strong, graceful man. His eyes were a cold blue and his long hair was a golden brown. A mustache hid his full upper lip. Women thought he was handsome—and clean. In an age when most people bathed once a week, Bill liked to take a daily bath.

After leaving the Free State Army Bill claimed some land near Monticello, Kansas. He earned his living by helping the local farmers. Elected town constable, Bill also made enemies. Twice someone burned his cabin while he was away.

Bill did not rebuild the cabin a third time. Instead he learned to drive a stagecoach. Before long he was an expert at controlling horses and mules with his long whip. Bill's first run was only fifty miles. From that point a second driver took over. When the next stage came by, Bill drove that one home.

The stage run was dull, hard work. Bill jumped at the chance to drive a freight wagon to Santa Fe, New Mexico. That was a run of 680 miles and full of adventure. The freight wagons carried goods for both traders and settlers. At night the drivers drew the wagons into a circle. Their oxen and horses grazed safely inside the circle.

Once Bill saw a driver hit a young boy. Bill was fond of children and he hated bullies. He knocked the man down. The boy told Bill his name was William Cody. Cody grew up to be the famous scout and showman, Buffalo Bill.

On another trip Bill heard a sound like thunder. He

soon saw that Indians had stampeded a herd of buffalo. The huge herd swept down on the wagon train. Bill set his brake and held the oxen still. As he had hoped the herd parted as it reached the wagons. Bill picked up his rifle and shot a big bull. That night he dined on buffalo meat for the first time.

On a trip to Santa Fe, Bill met one of his heroes. He was Kit Carson, the famous mountain man and explorer. The two men toured the town and danced in a cantina. Thanks to Carson's good advice, Bill left before the nightly fight broke out. Many good men had been killed in Santa Fe's drunken brawls.

Bill later took the dangerous job of driving a stage through the Rocky Mountains. On one trip his stage began slipping on ice at Raton Pass. All at once a runaway freight wagon came sliding down the hill toward him. Bill urged his mules into a trot. Somehow he kept the stage on the narrow, icy trail. As he safely skidded around a bend, the runaway wagon flew off the cliff.

Raton Pass was always treacherous. On a fine fall day in 1860 Bill's horse threw him when it was spooked by a female grizzly bear. The bear, who was protecting her cub, was on top of Bill before he could run. He fired his pistol into her huge body and slashed her with his knife. The maddened bear raked him with her sharp claws. With hope dying Bill plunged his knife deep into the bear's stomach.

A wagon driver found Bill lying beneath the dead bear. His scalp was torn and his left arm was crushed. A wagon carried him to Santa Fe. Doctors said he was sure to die, but Bill was tough. Sent back to Kansas City, he soon regained his health.

# 3

# THE CIVIL WAR YEARS

The Civil War began in April 1861. Bill wanted to join the struggle against slavery, but he was still laid up with his wounds. While his arm healed he worked at Rock Creek, Nebraska. That was the summer he killed Dave McCanles in a famous shootout. McCanles made the mistake of trying to bully Hickok. He also made threats against Horace Wellman, one of Bill's friends.

The trouble came to a head on July 12. When McCanles barged into Wellman's house, Bill told the bully to leave. McCanles refused. Bill nodded and stepped behind a curtain. McCanles did not know what to do next. At last McCanles stepped forward, his hand moving toward his gun. Bill fired through the curtain, hitting the big man in the chest. A jury said he fired in self-defense.

The Civil War was going badly for the North in the fall of 1861. Bill joined the Union Army in October and was put to work leading Army wagon trains. One trip took him to a town in Missouri. While he was there he saw a mob on its way to hang a friend of his. The quarry was a bartender who had wounded a gunman in a barroom brawl. Bill drew his pistol and aimed it at the mob's leaders. The hoodlums knew he meant what he said. They turned around and went off to find their fun elsewhere.

The town was soon buzzing with the news of Bill's brave stand. When he rode out of town, people cheered. A woman yelled, "Good for you, Wild Bill." From that time on he was always known as "Wild Bill."

Craving more excitement, Bill became a scout. His job was to find out what enemy troops were doing. That meant riding far behind the South's lines in southwest Missouri and Arkansas. For Bill it was a time of close calls and great adventures. As the stories were retold they became the stuff of legend.

On one trip Bill heard about a rebel captain who was carrying secret papers. Bill and two other scouts hid beside the road the captain would use. As the captain and his soldiers rode by, the scouts yelled and fired their pistols. The surprised rebels fled. Bill chased and caught the captain. With his knife he slit the man's coat open and found the papers.

Now Bill had to find his way back to the Union lines. As he rode northward he spotted four rebel soldiers outside a farm cabin. Two girls were cooking for them.

*Fighting during the Civil War was not confined to the battlefield. Rebel raiders looted and burned western towns that supported the Union.*

Bill captured the rebels and ate their lunch. He flirted with the girls and almost stayed too long. A second group of rebels rode up and opened fire. A bullet killed Bill's horse. He escaped when one of the girls gave him her horse.

Bill sometimes dressed in a rebel uniform. In Arkansas one summer he was arrested as a spy. A court-martial ordered him put to death. On the night before he was to die Bill managed to cut the ropes that bound him. Then he killed a guard and put on the guard's clothes. When the firing squad came in the morning Bill was gone.

In late 1863 Bill was carrying dispatches in an area controlled by Union forces. To his surprise he ran into a rebel raiding party. Bill shot two men and chased the third. The third man's horse was very fast, but Bill took a shortcut. When the two met, both fired at the same instant. The rebel missed, but Bill did not. He took the dead man's fine horse for his own use. The mare was strong, fast, and easy to train. Bill named her Black Nell.

After that Bill went back to Arkansas. He called himself Amos Jones and joined the South's army. That gave him a chance to listen in on rebel plans. In the spring of 1864 he was wounded while returning to Union lines. Once more his wound healed cleanly. He was soon off on more scouting trips.

The long war ended in April of 1865. Wild Bill was living in Springfield, Missouri, at the time. With nowhere else to go he stayed there. It was a rough town.

Many of the men had been soldiers, and most carried guns.

One of Bill's friends was a gambler named Dave Tutt. Bill borrowed money from Tutt and bought a saddle from him on credit. Almost without warning, Tutt began to cause trouble. Some people said it was because both men were courting Susanna Moore. She was probably the same girl who had given her horse to Bill during the war.

Both men liked to play poker. Because of Tutt's bad temper, Bill would not play with him. That made Tutt even more angry. When Bill played, Tutt would stand behind the other players and give them advice. He was clearly trying to start a fight.

Susanna warned Bill that Tutt planned to kill him in a gunfight. If it was a fair fight he would not go to jail. Bill told her he would not start a fight. Susanna believed him. She knew he would not run from one, either.

One night Tutt loaned $200 to a man who was playing against Bill. The cards ran against the man. Bill won all of the money. That was too much for Tutt. He asked Bill for the $40 he owed for the saddle. Bill handed him the money. Then Tutt said he wanted the $35 Bill owed him. Bill said it was only $25 and that he had a paper to prove it. Tutt picked up Bill's watch from the table. He said he would hold it until Bill came back with the paper. But Tutt was gone when Bill returned. So was the watch.

The two men came face-to-face in the town square on

*Very few men wanted to test Wild Bill's skill with a six-gun. Those who did often paid a high price. Dave Tutt challenged Bill to a shootout in 1865. Tutt's shot missed, but Bill's bullet killed the gambler. Here, Bill turns to ask if any of Tutt's friends want to try their luck.*

July 21, 1865. Bill knew that the gambler wanted a gunfight. Tutt was holding the watch in one hand and a pistol in the other. At a range of 75 yards, he pulled the trigger. The shot missed. Cool as always, Bill took aim. His bullet smashed into Tutt's heart.

As the crowd watched, Bill picked up his watch. Then he turned himself in to the sheriff. At the trial the jury said Bill shot in self-defense. Free once more he stayed in town for the rest of the year. Then he mounted Black Nell and headed toward Fort Riley, Kansas.

# 4

# LAWMAN AND INDIAN SCOUT

Wild Bill arrived at Fort Riley during the winter of 1866. The army post was in turmoil. Soldiers who hated military life were deserting. Some of them stole army horses and mules when they left.

Captain Richard Owen had sent for Bill. He asked his friend to become a deputy U.S. marshal. As a law officer Bill was in charge of restoring order at the fort. One big job was that of catching deserters and horse thieves. The salary for this dangerous work was only $75 a month.

Bill pinned on his lawman's star. Then he went after the latest mule thieves. He caught up with them two days later. When they saw it was Wild Bill they gave up without a fight. Bill took the thieves and the stolen mules back to Fort Riley.

With Wild Bill on duty desertions and thefts slowed down. Bill guided tourists across the plains in his spare

*A group of westerners pose outside a billiard hall. Wild Bill, dressed in his lawman's outfit, is standing fifth from the left. His fame as a gunslinger helped keep rowdy men like these from breaking the law.*

time. Dr. William Finlaw, the post doctor, also used Bill as a guide. Bill guarded Finlaw and his family when the doctor moved between forts. At night he slept under Finlaw's wagon to guard the children.

Early in the new year Bill tracked 200 stolen horses and mules to a distant valley. With the help of army scouts he took back the entire herd. Bill later said the outlaws were ready to fight for the valuable animals. That did not bother the lawmen. Their accurate rifle fire drove the thieves away.

Each week seemed to bring a new adventure. One day Bill spotted a runaway stagecoach. Urging Black

Nell into a gallop, he caught the speeding stage. As Nell kept pace he swung himself up to the driver's seat. Then he grabbed the reins and brought the horses to a stop. The frightened driver showed Bill that his hands were frozen. With Nell trotting behind, Bill drove the man to a doctor.

On a Saturday in 1868 Bill umpired a baseball game in Kansas City. The game matched the home team against a team from Atchison, Kansas. In those days baseball games often turned into riots. But no one dared

*Black Nell was Wild Bill's constant companion until her death in 1869. Here, she proves Bill's skill as a trainer by standing on a pool table. Bill relied on the mare's speed and endurance to pull out of many close scrapes.*

argue with this umpire's decisions. Kansas City won the high-scoring game, 48 to 28. As payment Bill was driven back to town in a carriage pulled by white horses.

This was the time of railroad building in the West. The first train had steamed into Fort Riley just before Wild Bill arrived. Now, as the steel rails moved westward, the Plains Indians fought to save their land.

General Winfield Scott Hancock was given the job of bringing peace to the plains. Wild Bill was not impressed. He said that General Hancock looked more at home behind a desk.

Hancock picked the headstrong George Armstrong Custer to lead the 7th Cavalry. Bill signed on as Custer's scout. He rode out ahead of the troops, looking for Indian camps and trails. Then he reported what he found to Custer.

When Custer sent messages to Fort Riley, it was Bill's job to carry them. Bill rode by night and hid by day, but the tactic sometimes failed. Once a raiding party of six warriors rode into the valley where Bill was hiding. Bill drew his pistols and fired, killing two. The others fled, but the shots brought more Indians to the scene. Only Nell's speed saved his scalp that day.

On another trip Bill was out on the plains when he heard the sound of running buffalo. Nell carried him away from the stampede—and into the path of three Indians. More braves soon joined the chase. Bill saw that Nell could not outrun them. He jumped down and told

*Dressed in his trademark buckskins, Wild Bill Hickok poses for a famous photo. In the Wild West, a scout who did not wear six-guns and a knife in his belt did not feel fully dressed.*

Nell to lie on her side. When the Indians closed in he opened fire. With three braves dead the others rode away.

The Indian wars dragged on. The army could not subdue the Plains tribes. General Hancock blamed Custer for the failure. A court-martial took Custer's command away from him.

In 1867 General Philip Sheridan replaced Hancock. Sheridan hoped to make a treaty with the Indian tribes gathered at Medicine Lodge. To keep the warriors peaceful the government gave them food and ammunition. Wild Bill thought that only madmen would give bullets to the Indians. Sure enough, the tribes soon were back on the warpath.

Sheridan recalled Custer to duty in 1868. He needed fighters and Custer was fearless. Wild Bill was still carrying messages. The work was not much fun. He was glad to learn that Sheridan was about to march. He wanted to be a scout again.

Wild Bill kept busy while he waited for the campaign to begin. He was leading a group of settlers one day when the Cheyenne attacked. After the settlers drove the Indians back with rifle fire, Bill pursued the retreating raiders. All at once three braves turned back and closed in on him. Bill fell with an arrow in his thigh. The Indians thought he was dead. When they moved in to scalp him he opened fire, killing all three. That night Bill rode through the Indian lines to bring help to the settlers.

The wound did not keep Wild Bill out of the saddle for long. On a trip out of Fort Lyon in 1869 he took a chance on riding by day. It was March and he knew the Indian ponies were in poor shape after a hard winter. At least one band of Cheyenne was far from winter camp, however. The braves saw his campfire and crept up on him. In a hand-to-hand fight Bill shot three Cheyenne. Then the war chief plunged a spear into Bill's hip. But Bill kept on shooting. He claimed later that all seven Indians were dead within a short time.

Bill pulled himself into the saddle and rode to Fort Lyon. A doctor shook his head as he cleaned the wound. Wild Bill's scouting days were over for a while.

*Wild Bill's exploits in the "Wild West" made exciting reading. Bill enjoyed his fame and talked freely to reporters. Most of the stories had a basis in fact, but often grew "taller" in the telling.*

27

# 5
# LAWLESS TOWNS NEED STRONG SHERIFFS

---

Hays City, Kansas, was founded in 1867. The town was one of the jumping off points for the Santa Fe Trail. Its warehouses held goods waiting to be carried westward.

The town was a violent place, even by the standards of the Old West. Hays City had no sheriff and no courts. Its two main streets were lined with saloons and dance halls. Gamblers and dance hall girls preyed on honest men. Drunken cowboys fired their pistols in the air. Murder and theft were daily events.

The townsfolk knew something had to be done. They sent their leaders to talk to Wild Bill. Would he help them clean up the town? Perhaps Bill was tired of Indian fighting. He took the job as acting sheriff of Ellis County in 1869.

When he lived in town Wild Bill dressed in fancy clothes. He traded his buckskins for a black coat and a wide-brimmed hat. A proud man, he wore handmade boots to show off his small feet. A red sash at his waist held two pearl-handled Colt pistols. To top off his outfit, Bill put on a cape lined with silk.

With Bill on the job the town settled down. But there were still hard, tough men in Hays City. Saloon owner Bill Curry was one of them. Wild Bill told Curry to fire

*As this invoice shows, Wild Bill earned $75 a month as sheriff of Hays City, Kansas. Hays City was located in Ellis County, which paid the lawman's salary. Although he was called by his nickname, he always signed his name J. B. Hickok.*

the crooked card dealers who worked for him. Curry did not take kindly to Bill's order. One day when Bill was playing cards, Curry put a pistol against Bill's head. All the card players froze. But Bill turned the threat into a joke. He laughed and offered to buy drinks for everyone. Curry shook Bill's hand and ended the feud.

Wild Bill's run-in with Jack Strawhun did not end as happily. Strawhun often bragged about the men he had killed. Once when Strawhun was fighting drunk, Bill helped tie him to a post. For that, Strawhun swore he would kill Wild Bill. The next time they met in a saloon Strawhun raised his pistol. Bill was ready and fired first. That night the town band played in their sheriff's honor.

The troops from Fort Hays also caused trouble. General Custer's brother Tom was one of the worst ruffians. Tom thought the general's fame would protect him. In July of 1870 Tom rode his horse into a billiard parlor. When the horse refused to jump over a table, he shot it. Bill then hauled the young man before a judge. Tom paid his fine, but swore he would get even.

A few nights later Tom's friends jumped Bill as he walked into a saloon. Bill shook them off and shot two before the rest fled. After they escaped the soldiers vowed vengeance. Bill's friends warned him that he could not fight the entire U.S. Army. Bill agreed that a dead sheriff would not be of much use. He packed his gear and took a train out of town.

Abilene, Kansas, at the end of the Chisholm Trail,

was the first great cowtown. Texas cowboys drove their herds of longhorn cattle north and sold them in Abilene. Then, with money in their pockets, they bathed and bought new clothes. They wore guns, for they would have felt undressed without them. Starved for fun, the cowboys played cards, danced, and drank rotgut whiskey. If they were not firing at the sky, they were shooting at each other.

In 1870 Tom Smith became Abilene's first marshal. He was murdered six months later. The next two marshals came and went even more quickly. In April of 1871 the mayor sent for Wild Bill. Bill looked around and said he would take the job. Abilene paid him $150 a month and 25 percent of the fines he collected.

In April Abilene was a quiet town of 500 people. Bill had time to learn his way around. The tracks divided the town in half. To the south were the saloons, gambling halls, and boarding houses. Homes, shops, and churches lay to the north.

The quiet vanished when the first herds arrived in May. By June, 7,000 people had crowded into town. Bill and his three deputies were busy night and day. It helped that no one was allowed to carry a gun in town. But enforcing the gun law in a town full of wild cowboys was far from easy.

One gunman who ignored the law was John Wesley Hardin. Young Hardin was said to have killed seven men on his way north from Texas. Ben Thompson, a saloon owner, tried to talk Hardin into killing Wild Bill. Hardin refused, saying he had no quarrel with Bill. He did insist on wearing his guns. When Bill saw the Texan he told Hardin to hand over his guns. Hardin did not want to shoot it out with Bill. He gave up his guns without a fight.

Bill tried hard to keep the gambling halls honest. He watched the games closely and cracked down on cheating. The owners vowed to get even. Bill guessed they would pay a gunman to kill him. To avoid ambush he

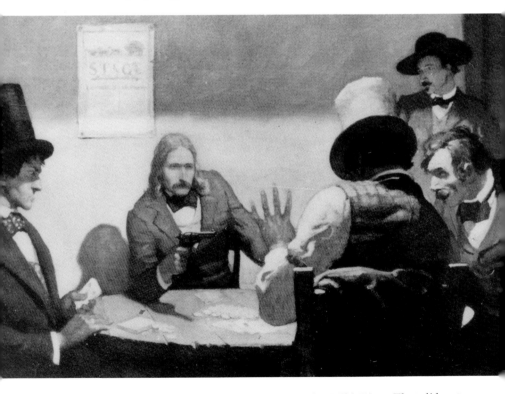

*Cheating in a poker game was common in the Wild West. That did not make it right, and Wild Bill disliked cheaters. Here, legend says he is telling the gambler, "I'm calling the hand that's in your hat."*

walked in the center of the street. He carried a shotgun and stayed clear of open doors. When he played cards he sat with his back to the wall. Lawmen who were careless died young.

Abilene always threw itself a party at the end of the year's cattle drives. Wild Bill set down only one rule: no shooting. The whiskey flowed and the crowd seemed to be having a noisy good time. Then Bill heard shooting outside the Alamo Saloon. He found Ben Thompson's partner, Phil Coe, with a gun in his hand. When Coe shot at him Bill returned the fire. Coe fell with two bullets in his stomach.

A second man ran toward Bill from the darkness. Bill fired again. A moment later he saw that he had killed Special Deputy Mike Williams. Mike was one of Bill's best friends.

The needless death upset Bill greatly. He could not forgive himself for killing a friend. That same night he turned in his badge. His career as a lawman was over.

# 6
## A SHOWMAN COMES TO THE END OF THE TRAIL

In the 1870s Wild West shows were all the rage. City people loved to watch cowboys and Indians. It helped if the show starred well-known western names. Wild Bill Hickok was one of the them. He was often featured in the magazines and dime novels of the day. When writers came to talk to him, Bill liked to tell tall tales about his life. Very often the stories grew taller and wilder in the telling.

Colonel Sidney Barnett hired Bill to put on a Wild West show in 1872. The show was booked for Niagara Falls, New York. Hotel owners were trying to attract more tourists to the falls. A Wild West show sounded like a great idea.

Wild Bill promised to put on a buffalo roundup. He soon found that shooting buffalo was easy compared to lassoing them. Once, when Bill roped a buffalo, it flipped his horse head over heels. In time Bill's men learned how to lasso buffalo by the horns. Then the big animals were shipped to New York by train. To Bill's dismay many died on the way.

The show ran for two days in August. Bill put on a fringed buckskin suit and announced the events. Cowboys chased and roped wild Texas steers. Then the buffalo were turned loose. Indians in warpaint chased them on fast mustangs. They shot blunt arrows at the buffalo. When the animals tired, the Indians roped them.

All agreed that it was a fine show. The crowd clapped for war dances, a lacrosse game, and music from a brass band. For real drama a dancing bear got loose and chased a sausage seller. In the end, the show failed because very few tickets were sold. Most of the crowd watched from behind a fence. Bill sold the buffalo and went back to the plains.

Wild Bill's show business career was reborn in 1873. Buffalo Bill Cody asked him to act in a stage play. Bill went to New York to play himself in *The Scouts of the Plains*. Ned Buntline, a dime novel writer, had dashed off the play in four hours. It was filled with Indian raids, captive maidens, and daring rescues.

Even though he was a terrible actor, Bill was a big hit. To New Yorkers he was a true western hero. The pay was good, but Bill said play acting was silly. In one scene the script called for him to drink some whiskey. Bill took a swig and spit it out. The bottle was full of tea, not

*Friends and showmen pose in costume for a rare photo. The three men in the center are (from left to right) Wild Bill, Buffalo Bill Cody, and Texas Jack Omohundro. The plays they appeared in were based on the real life exploits of these frontier scouts. Wild Bill always played himself on stage.*

whiskey. Bill roared, "Either I get real whiskey or I ain't tellin' no story."

The play toured eastern cities for six months. Day by day Wild Bill's temper grew shorter. He hated the spotlight and one night he shot it out with his pistol. On stage he played tricks on Buffalo Bill and the other cast members. The night came at last when Bill could not take any more. He took off his costume and walked away. His last words were, "I ain't going to do it any more."

Wild Bill returned to the western plains. For a time he and Buffalo Bill served as guides for rich English hunters. This was a restless time for Bill. He lived in the Wyoming Territory for a while. His friends knew that his vision was fading. Some thought his eyes had been

36

injured by an exploding footlight. Proud as always, Bill did not like to talk about the problem.

In the spring of 1876 Wild Bill married a widow named Agnes Lake Thatcher. There had been other women in his life, but he had never settled down. Bill had first met Agnes, who owned a circus, five years earlier in Abilene. The romance had flickered off and on. Now, at last, they were man and wife.

The couple spent their honeymoon at Agnes's home in Ohio. Then Bill left his bride and went off to hunt for gold. He was hoping to strike it rich in the Black Hills of the Dakota Territory. A man needed money to make a home for a new wife.

*Wild Bill did not marry until 1876. His bride was Agnes Lake Thatcher, a widowed circus owner. After his death Agnes wrote, "It is impossible for a human being to love any better than what I did him."*

Wild Bill was always ready to make a deal. He and Charlie Utter agreed to start a Black Hills transport line. While Utter worked on the details, Bill rode on to Deadwood in what is now South Dakota. The raw mining town was a rough, lawless place. Bill spent his days there searching for gold.

In Deadwood Bill crossed paths with Martha Jane Canary. Men knew her better as Calamity Jane. Calamity dressed in men's clothes, smoked cigars, and ran a mining claim. She had a crush on Bill and talked about him all the time. Even though Bill was married she proposed that they should "join up." There is no proof that Bill returned Calamity's love. In fact, he stayed away from her when he could.

The outlaws and gamblers of Deadwood were worried. If Wild Bill became marshal, he would clean up the town. Bill did not want to be a lawman again. But he did not back away from a fight. One night six gunmen threatened to kill him. Bill whipped out his guns and backed the men against a wall. Calmly he told them to shut their mouths. "If you don't," he promised, "Deadwood will see some cheap funerals."

Tim Brady and Johnny Varnes were two of Bill's enemies. They wanted to kill Wild Bill, but they were afraid of him. The safe way was to hire someone to do the job. A local tough named Jack McCall was their man. Brady told him he would be famous if he killed Bill

*Martha Jane Canary was better known as Calamity Jane. She fell in love with Wild Bill when they met on the way to Deadwood. Bill may have admired her spirit, but he did not lose his heart to her. Calamity later made a false claim that she was the mother of Bill's child. She also asked to be buried near him.*

*In 1876, the Black Hills gold fields were filled with men eager to strike it rich. Wild Bill lived in a make-shift camp such as this while he was in Deadwood. As the miner guarding his tent with a rifle suggests, these were lawless times.*

Hickok. To sweeten the deal the partners gave McCall a bag of gold dust.

On August 2, 1876, Bill was playing poker in a saloon. He felt nervous because he did not have his back to the wall. As Bill studied his cards, McCall walked up behind him. The gunman raised his pistol and cried, "Take that!" Then, at close range, he fired at Bill's head.

Wild Bill slumped to the floor. His dead fingers were holding a pair of aces, a pair of eights, and a jack. Poker players who are dealt those cards still call them "the dead man's hand."

*Miners, gamblers and saloon keepers fill Deadwood's single main
street. Deadwood was a boom town that grew up almost overnight. It
was in the town's No. 10 saloon that Jack McCall shot Wild Bill.*

# 7

# THE LEGEND OF WILD BILL

Jack McCall did not live long enough to enjoy his sudden fame. After the shooting he tried to hide in a butcher shop. Some say it was Calamity Jane who dragged him out to stand trial. At the trial McCall claimed that Bill had shot his younger brother. The jury believed him and found him not guilty. The killer fled from Deadwood before Bill's friends could catch him.

Four weeks later McCall was arrested in Laramie, Wyoming. He had been bragging that he had killed the great Wild Bill. A judge ruled that the first trial did not count. A second jury found McCall guilty of murder. He was hanged three months later.

The name of Wild Bill's killer soon faded, but Bill's name lives on. Unlike many western heroes Bill was well known during his lifetime. If some of the stories were more myth than fact, Bill's skill with a gun was real. A magazine called him "the Prince of Pistoleers."

Wild Bill was only thirty-nine when he died. In that short life he was a Civil War hero, army scout, lawman, showman, and guide. He loved children and kept in close touch with his family. Would he have been a good husband and father? Death came too soon to know.

There were those who said Wild Bill was too quick on the trigger. Others said he was a crude and violent man. George Custer defended his friend. He wrote, "Whether on foot or on horseback he was one of the

*During the late 1800s the public was eager to read about its western heroes. Writers were happy to fill that demand. Some knew the West and its people, but many did not. Safe in the East, they created fanciful stories about Wild Bill and other gunslingers. Today, their stories make it hard to separate fact from fiction when we study the Wild West.*

*Colorado Charlie Utter held a funeral for Wild Bill and put up a grave marker. Here he kneels beside the grave of his friend and partner. The message above Charlie's name reads, "Pard, we will meet again in the happy hunting grounds to part no more. Goodbye."*

most perfect types of physical manhood I ever saw . . . [M]any are the personal quarrels . . . he has checked . . . by [saying] 'This has gone far enough.' "

In 1929 the state of Illinois put up a monument at Wild Bill's birthplace. A bronze tablet says that Wild Bill helped make the West "a safe place for women and children." Bill would have been proud of that tribute.

# GLOSSARY

**Border Ruffians**—Raiders from Missouri who tried to make Kansas a slave state in the years before the Civil War.

**Civil War**—The war between the North and South, 1861–1865.

**court-martial**—A trial conducted by a military court.

**desertion**—The act of running away from one's military unit.

**dime novels**—Low-cost magazines that printed popular fiction during the late 1800s.

**Free State Army**—An armed force set up in Kansas to combat the Border Ruffians from Missouri.

**gunslingers**—Outlaws and lawmen of the Wild West who settled arguments with their pistols.

**jury**—A group of people sworn to judge the facts and give a verdict in a court case.

**lacrosse**—An Indian game in which players catch and pass a ball using long-handled sticks with a webbed pouch at the end.

**myth**—A story that many people believe, but which is almost always untrue.

**rebels**—A name for the people and soldiers of the South during the Civil War.

**scout**—Someone who goes out ahead of the army to study the enemy's positions.

**stampede**—A sudden, headlong rush of startled animals.

**town constable**—A lawman who keeps the town's peace.

**Underground Railroad**—The system of "safe" houses, used before the Civil War, to help runaway slaves escape to Canada.

**Union Army**—The name given to the United States forces that fought against the rebel army of the South during the Civil War.

# MORE GOOD READING
# ABOUT WILD BILL HICKOK

Anderson, A. M. *Wild Bill Hickok*. New York: Harper & Row, 1947.

Connelley, William Elsey. *Wild Bill and His Era*. Savage, Md.: Cooper Square, 1972.

Drago, Harry Sinclair. "Wild Bill Takes Charge," in *The Legend Makers*. New York: Dodd, Mead & Co., 1975, pp. 22–34.

Fielder, Mildred. *Wild Bill and Deadwood*. Superior, Wis.: Superior Publishing Co., 1965.

Garst, Shannon. *Wild Bill Hickok*. New York: Julian Messner, 1952.

Horan, James D. "Wild Bill Hickok," in *The Authentic Wild West: the Gunfighters*. New York: Crown Publishers, 1977, pp. 81–122.

Rosa, Joseph G. *The West of Wild Bill Hickok*. Norman, Okla.: University of Oklahoma Press, 1982.

Rosa, Joseph G. *They Called Him Wild Bill*. Norman, Okla.: University of Oklahoma Press, 1974.

# INDEX

shootouts, 15, 19–20,
30, 33, 38
as showman, 34–36
as stagecoach driver,
12–14
stops runaway stage-
coach, 22–23
wounded, 13–14, 18,
26, 27
youth, 8–11
Hickok, Lorenzo (brother), 10
Hickok, Oliver (brother), 10
Hickok, Polly (mother), 8, 10
Hickok, William (father), 8–
9, 10
Homer, Illinois, 8

**K**

Kansas City, Kansas, 14, 23-
24

**L**

Lane, Colonel James, 5, 7, 11

**M**

McCall, Jack, 38, 40, 42
Monticello, Kansas, 12
Moore, Susanna, 19

**N**

Niagara Falls, New York,
34–35

**O**

Owen, Captain Richard, 21

**R**

Raton Pass, 13

**S**

Sante Fe, New Mexico, 12
*Scouts of the Plains, The*, 35
Sheridan, Gen. Philip, 26
Smith, Tom, 31
Strawhun, Jack, 30

**T**

Thatcher, Agnes Lake
(wife), 37
Thompson, Ben, 31–33
Tutt, Dave, 19–20

**U**

Underground Railroad, 9
Utter, Charlie, 38, *44*

**W**

Wild West show, 34–35
Williams, Mike,  33